THE HIDDEN ROOTS OF AIKIDO

Sokaku Takeda.

THE HIDDEN ROOTS OF AIKIDO

AIKI JUJUTSU DAITORYU

Shiro Omiya

KODANSHA INTERNATIONAL
Tokyo • New York • London

NOTES TO THE READER:

Macrons are used for Japanese terms throughout this book; the few exceptions are based on custom and mainly involve people's names.

Many techniques described in *The Hidden Roots of Aikido* are dangerous and should be attempted only under the supervision of a master Daitoryu practitioner. The publisher is not responsible for injuries that result from readers' practice of any of these techniques.

Originally published as *Shinden Aiki Kōketsu Ōhi* (Tokyo: Hachiman Shoten, 1992).

Jacket photo by Naoto Suzuki.

Distributed in the United States by Kodansha America, Inc., 575 Lexington Avenue, New York, New York 10022, and in the United Kingdom and continental Europe by Kodansha Europe Ltd., 95 Aldwych, London WC2b 4JF.

Published by Kodansha International, Ltd., 17-14 Otowa 1-chome, Bunkyo-ku, Tokyo 112-8652, and Kodansha America, Inc.

First edition, 1998
99 00 01 02   10 9 8 7 6 5 4 3 2

ISBN 4-7700-2327-8

Library of Congress CIP data available

CONTENTS

PREFACE

Recent years have seen an upsurge of interest in the Daitoryu, a controversial martial art considered to be one of the primary sources of Aikido, a modern discipline popular the world over. One prominent Daitoryu master instructor has described this martial art tradition in these terms:

> Unlike most systems, the Daitoryu is wholly martial in character. And in the Daitoryu, we never assume that a battle will be simply one against one; all the subtle techniques presuppose attacks coming from all sides. The Daitoryu is a preeminently practical and efficient system.

The Daitoryu is an extremely efficient martial art system, but execution of its techniques does not depend on size or physical strength. This is amply demonstrated by the example of Sokaku Takeda (1860–1943), a thin little man who nevertheless was the dominant martial artist of the early twentieth century. Sokaku regularly defeated all comers—including sumo wrestlers and experts in judo, karate, or kendo—until he was well into his eighties. The source of his amazing skill was his mastery of *aiki*, the essence of the Daitoryu system. Another important element in the unique Daitoryu system is its inclusion of ancient Shinto teachings and esoteric practices that dramatically increase practitioners' knowledge of the cosmos and their capacity to utilize universal energy to its fullest.

This book is an introduction to the Daitoryu system of teachings that were kept secret for many centuries and that were expressed in various forms, including written texts, person-to-person transmission, and oral instruction. I hope that it will afford the reader a glimpse into the fascinating world of the Daitoryu martial art tradition.

Sokaku Takeda in his later years.

PART
I

DAITORYU:
AN OVERVIEW

Historical Development of the Tradition

THE DAITORYU is believed to have originated within the family of Emperor Seiwa (reigned A.D. 858–876) and to have been greatly developed by one of the emperor's descendants, Shinra Saburo Minamoto no Yoshimitsu, in the eleventh century. Through his careful study of human anatomy—he made a point of visiting battlefields and execution grounds to examine and dissect the bodies of war dead and executed criminals—Yoshimitsu determined which were the most effective strikes, blows, holds, joint locks, and pins. To fathom the mysteries of *aiki*, or harmonized energy, Yoshimitsu spent hours observing a female spider trapping prey in her

Samurai commander Shinra Saburo Minamoto no Yoshimitsu playing the *sho*.

web. Furthermore, he was a talented musician, and while accompanying dancers on his *sho* (a type of wind instrument), he gained insight into the nature of good rhythm and smooth transition between movements. Yoshimitsu incorporated all of this knowledge into the martial art he had been taught by family members and then passed on to his sons this improved and expanded system—which came to be known as the "Daitoryu," after the name of one of his residences.

Yoshikiyo, his eldest son, settled in the village of Takeda in Koma (in present-day Yamanashi Prefecture) and founded the Takeda branch of the Minamoto clan. The Daitoryu tradition of Yoshimitsu was thereafter handed down in complete secrecy to successive generations of the Takeda family. Near the end of the sixteenth century, the family, led by Kunitsugu Takeda, shifted its main base to the Aizu district (in present-day Fukushima Prefecture). There the martial art system became known as *o-shiki-uchi*, or "practice in the room," and alternatively as an *o-tome-bujutsu*, or "inside-the-clan martial art"; both these terms are thought to suggest the great secrecy with which the Daitoryu techniques were guarded. The art was secretly transmitted to the samurai of the Aizu domain until the fall of the Shogunate in 1868.

It was not until the nineteenth century—when martial art genius Sokaku Takeda began to teach the Daitoryu to the public—that the art became widely known. Sokaku was born in 1860 in Aizu, where he received instruction in the traditional *o-shiki-uchi* arts of the Aizu clan from his relatives and from Tanomo Saigo (1830–1905), the last minister of the Aizu domain. Sokaku is considered the thirty-fifth Grand Master of the Daitoryu tradition stemming from Kunitsugu Takeda. In addition to the Daitoryu system, Sokaku studied many other martial arts and acquired firsthand combat experience in street fights all over the country. Around the turn of the century, Sokaku began teaching the Daitoryu system—which by then included some new elements that he himself had incorporated—to select groups of military officers, police officials, and aristocrats. Sokaku was based in remote northern Japan but made occasional forays to Tokyo and western Japan. In the course of his travels, Sokaku defeated all challengers. It is said that thirty thousand martial artists received instruction at Sokaku's hands. Of this vast number, only twenty or so received formal teaching licenses from the Daitoryu Grand Master. Several of Sokaku's students themselves became extremely distinguished teachers.

Tanomo Saigo.

Sokaku Takeda.

Yukiyoshi Sagawa (1902–1998) was one of Sokaku's earliest students. He began studying with Sokaku in Hokkaido when he was just twelve years old, and continued this training for many years. Sagawa eventually settled in Kodaira, a suburb of Tokyo, and established a *dōjō* (training hall) there. Sagawa was widely considered to be the premier Daitoryu exponent of the second half of the twentieth century.

Another early student of the Daitoryu was Kodo Horikawa (1895–1980). Horikawa began his training in Daitoryu under his father, one of Sokaku's first students, and then with the Grand Master himself. Horikawa lived all his life in Hokkaido's Kitami district, where he disseminated the Daitoryu teachings. He had many excellent students, the foremost of whom is Seigo Okamoto (1925–).

Takuma Hisa (1896–1980) was Sokaku's principal student in western Japan. He is believed to be the only one of Sokaku's students to have received the complete

Ryōzen Shrine, where then–chief priest Tanomo Saigo initiated Sokaku Takeda into the secrets of the Daitoryu.

Takuma Hisa.

transmission of all the Daitoryu techniques for unarmed and armed combat. After university, where he had been a champion sumo wrestler, he taught Aiki Jujutsu Daitoryu for many years in and around Osaka. He taught a great many students. Hakaru Mori (1931–) and other of his most outstanding students continue to teach Hisa-style Daitoryu in the Kansai region.

Tokimune Takeda (1916–1993), Sokaku's second son, established a Daitoryu *aiki budō* headquarters in Abashiri, Hokkaido in 1953, subsequently assuming leadership of the Daitoryu tradition. In this role, Tokimune established an archive for Daitoryu-related material, codified all of the Daitoryu techniques, and established branch *dōjō* throughout Japan. Tokimune Takeda's principal student, Katsuyuki Kondo (1945–), is active promoting Daitoryu *aiki budo* in the Tokyo area.

Morihei Ueshiba (1883–1969) was Sokaku's most famous student. Morihei first met Sokaku in 1915 in Hokkaido, and trained under him until 1922, when Morihei in turn was licensed to teach. Under the influence of Onisaburo Deguchi (1871–1948), charismatic leader of the Ōmoto-kyō religion, Morihei adopted and simplified the Daitoryu techniques and added a prominent spiritual dimension to create the art of Aikido—which in recent years has become extremely well known around the world and gained a large international following.

The Daitoryu tradition continues in various forms in Japan, and its teachings are slowly being introduced to the rest of the world.

Morihei Ueshiba.

Theory

THE CONCEPT OF *AIKI* (harmonized energy), central to both the Daitoryu and Aikido, is extremely ancient. Clear reference to the techniques of *aiki* can be found in the eighth-century *Kojiki*, Japan's earliest chronicle, which includes the tale of Take-mi-kazuchi-no-kami and Take-mi-nakata-no-kami. These two Shinto deities were both known for their tremendous strength, and eventually the inevitable contest between them occurred. When Take-mi-nakata grabbed the wrist of Take-mi-kazuchi, Take-mi-kazuchi's arm turned first into a pillar of ice and then into a sword blade, causing Take-mi-nakata to recoil in awe. Then when Take-mi-kazuchi grabbed his opponent's wrist, he crushed it like a young reed, causing Take-mi-nakata to concede defeat and flee in terror. Similarly, masters of *aiki* know how to turn their arm into an iron staff and their hand into a sword blade; they are also able to apply techniques such as *yonka-jō* to crush an opponent's wrist.

The concept of *ki* (life force) is familiar to students of Chinese qigong, who call this same energy *ch'i* or *qi*. Every culture has a similar word for the harmonizing principle of universal energy that animates all existence, or the vibrant force that activates life. In ancient Rome, it was *aura*; in India, it was *prana*; in Japan prior to World War II, it was *reiki* or *reishi*. Shamans and mediums are believed to be particularly sensitive to the flow of *ki*. In its concentrated form, *ki* may be perceived as light, which explains why seers and saints like the Buddha or Christ are often depicted with haloes—divine light can actually be seen if one is perceptive enough.

This kind of perceptiveness is not simply a matter of acquiring knowledge of a person by closely observing his actions, listening to his words, and letting his character rub off on you; it is rather an actual and direct sensation of *ki*. Masters with a true understanding of *ki* can accomplish such seemingly miraculous feats as curing mental and physical illness, exorcising malevolent spirits, communicating telepathically, or, in the realm of martial arts, downing an opponent without even touching him.

In addition, *ki* has the power to pacify. The chapter in the *Kojiki* on Emperor

Sujin states, "The divine spirit (*shinki*) will not arise to your harm and the land will be made tranquil," and in the *Nihon Shoki* we find, "Attain the divine spirit, and all will bow down before you." The following passage is found in *Shin'ihō*, an early text on ancient Japanese medicine compiled by Tanba no Yasuyori (912–95):

> Within the human body the heavenly elements of fire, *ki*, earth, and water function together harmoniously. Whatever disrupts that balance is called "sickness." The eight ways and methods to restore that balance are called "medicine." All cures begin with the harmonization of water *ki* and fire *ki*.

The importance of *ki* is stressed again and again in Chinese philosophy. The *Pao-P'u-Tzu* (known in Japanese as *Hōbokushi*), a seventh-century collection of Taoist texts, states:

> *Ki* is inside and outside every human being, and there is nothing in this heaven or earth of ours that lacks *ki*.

Ki is the basis of creation and the determining factor of existence. Without *ki*, there can be no life.

> In order to obtain immortality, an adept must treasure the body's essential fluids, foster *ki*, and partake of elixirs.

According to the *Pao-P'u-Tzu*, fostering *ki* is one of the three preconditions for immortality. Fostering *ki* (which includes breath control techniques) allows an adept to conquer all illness, pacify wild animals, walk on water, and attain great longevity.

The study and practice of *ki* has always been important in Asian culture. More specifically in Japanese Shinto, many esoteric practices handed down from ancient times are designed to enlighten human beings to the true nature of *ki*—to the way *ki* functions throughout the universe and the way its power may be harnessed.

In the very beginning of the *Kojiki*, the two deities of creation, Takami-musubi (representing the yang principle) and Kami-musubi (representing the yin principle), employed the marvelous power of *musubi* (creative energy) to bring the world into being. Likewise, the functioning of *musubi* can be seen in the techniques of *aiki*, in which one blends one's *ki* with that of a partner, or attempts to link one's individual *ki* with the universal *ki*. In Shinto, *ki no musubi* is the generative force of all life; in *aiki* martial arts, it is the origin of myriad techniques. Even without knowledge of the most basic martial art techniques, a person can still evade an opponent's thrusts and grabs from any direction if he or she is enlightened to the principles of blending *ki*.

The fostering of *ki* and the harnessing of *musubi* creative power are not just for Taoist wizards and Shinto sages but are key factors in the training of martial artists. Breathing that is not smooth and controlled has an adverse effect on one's body and mind; conversely, good breath control enhances ordinary strength considerably. Breath control is mandatory for mastery of the martial arts; all serious students do breath control exercises daily. In *aiki budō* systems such as the Daitoryu, movement of the hands—upward and downward, in and out—always requires and incorporates applied breath control; clear definition and understanding of these principles is essential to the development of *ki* power.

In a truly spiritual experience, control of *ki* and *musubi* allows the practitioner to perceive the real nature of existence and the functioning of the universe; only those with such profound perception are capable of harnessing the power of universal *ki*. By means of their mastery of this spiritual power, Taoist wizards, Tantric masters, and Shinto sages are said to be able to protect human beings from natural disasters, heal the sick, produce pills of immortality, create happiness for all, and pacify the earth.

In Tantrism and Yoga, various *mudra* (hand signs) and *asana* (yogic postures) are employed to utilize universal energy. In *aiki budō* as well, various internal and external techniques are employed to foster the development of *ki* power. In order to utilize *ki*, one must understand certain principles and specific forms; when the true principles and their physical manifestations are experienced, movements can be transformed, leading eventually to total integration of body and mind, or self and cosmos. For example, in the *aiki-age* technique (lifting an opponent off the ground to break his balance), the simple act of forming the *chinkon mudra* and calming the spirit makes it much easier to perform the technique well. Of course, merely forming the *mudra* does not ensure full generation of *ki* power, but it does make it easier to concentrate and direct energy.

At present, practitioners of *aiki*-related systems often speak of "downing an opponent with *aiki*" or "using *aiki* to immobilize an opponent," but each system has a slightly different emphasis, reflected in the respective theoretical and technical approaches employed. One common approach in *aiki* systems is the principle of "using

Chinkon mudra.

techniques that neutralize an opponent's power." By applying such techniques, *aiki* practitioners—whether men, women, or children—can overcome the strength of even a much more powerful opponent.

Another approach is based on the principle of "blending your *ki* with that of your opponent and linking yourself to the cosmos." Proper execution of such advanced techniques requires a high level of enlightenment but, once mastered, these remarkable techniques enable human beings to disarm their foes and to eliminate aggression, sometimes even on a universal scale. The question of whether or not the principle of cosmic harmony and a desire for world peace are implicit in the Daito-ryu teachings remains a matter for debate, but Morihei Ueshiba, strongly influenced by the spiritual teachings of the Ōmoto-kyō sect of Shinto, made the quest for world peace a central pillar of Aikido.

In the martial arts, *aiki* exists simultaneously with *kiai*. The term *kiai* is often explained and used in a variety of ways, but it can be broadly taken to mean being inspired to act with *ki*; every system stresses its importance. (*Kiai* is both a state of mind and a physical form, manifested as a spirited yell.) It is said that with good *kiai* a weight lifter can increase the amount he is able to lift by as much as fifteen percent.

The renowned kendo master Sasaburō Takano once wrote:

> *Kiai* must be fostered constantly. The fostering of *kiai* is the fostering of the spirit. *Kiai* is the harmonization of one *ki* with another *ki*, the blending of two spiritual forces. Use *ki* to strike *ki*.

Anyone who truly grasps this principle may be able to control an opponent without even touching him, and there have in fact been martial art masters who have displayed this remarkable ability. Their mastery of *ki* allowed them entry to a higher spiritual realm.

Basic Training Methods

Standing and Seated Forms

IN THE PRACTICE OF A TECHNIQUE, the action revolves around an *uke* (the person who initiates an attack and then receives the response) and a *tori* (the one who takes action against an attack and then neutralizes it). A technique can be practiced in any of three different forms: with both partners standing; with one partner seated and one partner standing; or with both sitting. The same technique is executed differently in each of the three forms, and it is good to practice all three forms for each technique. All techniques presented in this book can be practiced in any of the three forms, thus tripling the number of possible techniques.

Each form presents a different challenge regarding stance and *ma-ai* (combative distance between *tori* and *uke*), and each *aiki*-related martial arts system explains these challenges and describes the execution of a technique in different ways; so

The three forms in which techniques can be practiced.

there is no one set pattern. Aiki Jujutsu, like other traditional Japanese martial arts, places comparatively little importance on *kamae* (combative stance); however, most *aiki*-related martial art systems maintain that good posture is key to the proper execution of techniques. Acquisition of good posture requires considerable trial and error, but techniques cannot be executed without it. In general, the Daitoryu Jujutsu method emphasizes stability, application of full power, and large stepping movements, while Aiki no Jutsu systems rely less on physical power, and more on timing and on smaller steps.

A good combative distance is one that allows you to negate your opponent's power while fostering your own. Again, such a skill can only be learned from practical experience dealing with large and small opponents, unarmed and armed attacks, and punches and kicks.

Let us take a look at the special characteristics of each of the three forms. In seated techniques the basic posture is *seiza* (kneeling with the back held straight), which is very solid and stable. The lower half of the body is firmly rooted to the ground while the upper half can be projected upwards with much power. Movement in seated techniques is accomplished by "knee-walking," an exercise that greatly increases the strength and flexibility of the legs and hips. In standing techniques you learn how to move freely in any direction—forward, sideways, backward—and guide the opponent. One-seated-one-standing techniques combine the solidity of seated techniques with the flexibility of standing techniques. The techniques in this form stretch from heaven to earth. It appears that the partner standing has a great advantage when he attacks with a blow to the head or attempts a two-handed grab, but in fact the partner who is seated can neutralize the attack with relative ease by means of good posture and simple movements. The practice of one-seated-one-standing techniques such as *shihō-nage* and *aiki-nage* are valuable for beginners because they teach good posture and solid movement.

The Three Methods: Daitoryu Jujutsu, Daitoryu Aiki Jujutsu, and Daitoryu Aiki no Jutsu

Just as the same technique can be practiced in three forms—standing, one-seated-one-standing, or sitting—there are three distinct methods of applying a technique and controlling an opponent: the Daitoryu Jujutsu method of relying primarily on *atemi* (blows or kicks to any of the body's pressure points); the Daitoryu Aiki Jujutsu method of combining *atemi* with *aiki* timing; and the Daitoryu Aiki no Jutsu method of relying mainly on *aiki* timing.

Daitoryu Jujutsu is geared toward younger practitioners. *Atemi* is applied full force, and the joints are attacked with simple, straightforward vigor. These techniques are good for basic training. Daitoryu Aiki Jujutsu techniques, combining *atemi* and *aiki* timing, are suitable for older practitioners. The emphasis is less on devastating control of an opponent, and more on complicated pins that stretch an opponent's joints and limbs—a kind of martial yoga. In contrast to the forceful counterattacks and firm pins of the first two methods, Daitoryu Aiki no Jutsu techniques reduce movement to a minimum and control an opponent with spiritual rather than physical power. This is the essence of the Daitoryu; techniques like *aiki-age* are especially effective in helping the practitioner develop skill in this area.

Let us look at *ippon-dori*, the most basic of techniques, executed in each of the three methods:

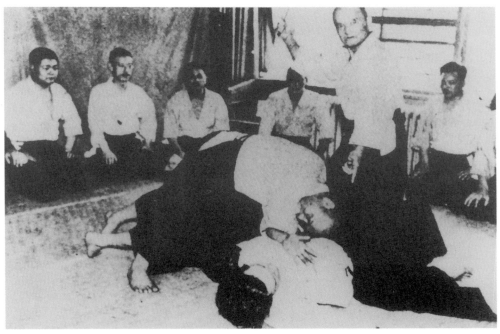

This 1936 photo shows Sokaku Takeda after he has thrown several opponents.

Daitoryu Jujutsu *Ippon-dori*

As *uke* strikes with his right hand, *tori* responds by grabbing the *kyokuchi* and *shōkai* pressure points near his opponent's elbow and the *yōkei* and *yōkoku* pressure points near the wrist. After bending *uke*'s arm, *tori* strikes *uke*'s ribs with his left fist and then follows this with a kick to the same place. *Tori* drops *uke* to the mat facedown, pins *uke*'s right arm with his leg, and delivers an elbow strike to the *godenkō* pressure point on the neck. As can be seen here, *jujutsu* involves employing overwhelming force to attack an opponent's weak points and to subdue him with blows and locks.

Daitoryu Aiki Jujutsu *Ippon-dori*

As soon as *uke* attacks with his right hand, *tori* slides in on his left leg and blocks the attack with his right hand, simultaneously applying *atemi* to *uke*'s ribs. *Tori* grabs *uke*'s wrist and elbow and drives the arm back toward *uke*'s face. *Tori* then slides in on his right leg and, by controlling the elbow, pins *uke* to the mat.

4

5

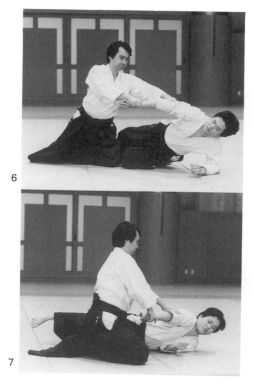

6

7

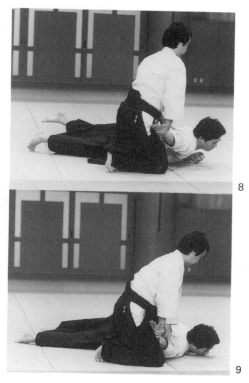

8

9

Daitoryu Aiki no Jutsu *Ippon-dori*

As *uke* strikes with his right hand, *tori* rises up in *aiki-age*, grabs *uke*'s underarm and wrist, then brings him to the mat in front of *tori*'s *hara* (center of gravity). Note that in the execution of this technique *tori*'s movement is kept to a minimum, and the grip on *uke*'s wrist differs from that used in the above two methods. Practitioners should be aware of the different set of principles functioning in each form.

Basic Training Methods Using Specific Techniques

Every martial art system stresses the development of arm and elbow power and strong finishing movements. In the Daitoryu, stability of the hips and legs and good posture is also very important. In medieval times, many battles were conducted on horseback and a high-ranking warrior needed to be able to use both hands and legs equally well in order to control a horse and wield a weapon simultaneously. The samurai of the Aizu domain were said to be especially good at incorporating the movements of everyday life in the castle—sitting, standing, walking—into their martial art training.

The basic stance in Daitoryu is the "horseback riding posture," with the body facing forward, feet spread and arms at the sides, as if one were riding a horse into battle. This is a natural, stable posture also commonly employed in Chinese martial arts, where it is said to aid in the free flow of *ki*.

The following basic training methods are good for facilitating full use of the hands when moving, and for helping to improve stability of the hips and legs. Other basic techniques such as *ikka-jō*, *nika-jō*, *sanka-jō*, *kote-gaeshi*, and *shihō-nage* differ in detail, but operate on the same fundamental principles.

Basic Training Using *Irimi-nage*

Tori stands in right *hanmi* with both hands extended. *Uke* firmly grabs *tori*'s right arm with both hands. *Tori* steps forward on first the right leg and then the left, and relaxes his shoulders while keeping his head and shoulders up. *Tori* then pivots 180 degrees on his right foot, sweeping the left leg around while holding *uke*'s elbow. After planting both feet solidly on the ground *tori* releases his grip on *uke*'s arm, holds *uke*'s head with his left hand, and straightens up. *Tori* lifts his right arm, cradles *uke*'s head in his arms, and then steps forcefully behind *uke*, bringing his right arm down to effect the throw.

Basic Training Using *Yonka-jō*

Tori stands in right *hanmi* with both hands extended. *Uke* firmly grabs *tori*'s right arm with both hands. *Tori* takes a step forward with his right leg, raising his right hand in a slight spiraling motion, and then pivots 180 degrees on his right foot to align himself to *uke*'s right. *Tori* turns his hand to loosen *uke*'s grasp and rotates *uke*'s palm outwards. *Tori* applies *yonka-jō*, aligns his feet, then takes a step forward on his right leg while cutting downward with both hands, applying pressure to *uke*'s wrist with his right hand to bring him to the ground and pin him. (Keeping *uke*'s arm slightly off the ground here is more effective.)

Basic Training Using *Shihō-nage*

Tori stands in right *hanmi* with both hands extended. *Uke* grabs both of *tori*'s wrists. *Tori* shifts his feet diagonally to the right and spreads his fingers, keeping his hands directly in front of his own center. *Tori* then steps in with his left leg, raising his hands high above his head; *uke* follows the movement, which brings him back-to-back with *tori*. *Tori* brings both arms down, causing *uke* to "float" on his toes, facing the opposite direction. *Tori* reassumes a stable right *hanmi* stance.

Aiki Jūmon and the Eight-Direction Throw

I have organized *aiki* techniques into ten different dimensions (*jūmon*). Here I would like to discuss two of the principal dimensions: *aiki-age* (also called "fire-dragon movement") and *aiki-sage* ("water-dragon movement").

My approach to the Daitoryu incorporates the secret teaching of "immovable movement" (*fudō no dō*). "Immovable" here refers to the idea of being "firmly centered" or "securely grounded," a state in which it is possible to move all other elements. The term "immovable" can also mean being "unperturbed," or keeping oneself unmoved by external conditions and thus capable of handling any attack. But no matter how expertly a technique maybe explained, real understanding can come only from practical experience and direct instruction.

The secret of *aiki-age* is *fudō daiji*: keeping the thumbs as the immovable focal point, the wrists, arms, and shoulders are turned upward in a circular motion to make an opponent rise up on his toes, causing him to lose his balance. The secret of *aiki-sage* is *fudō shōji*: in this technique, the little fingers form the immovable center and the wrists, arms, and shoulders turn downward in a circular motion until the opponent's posture is broken.

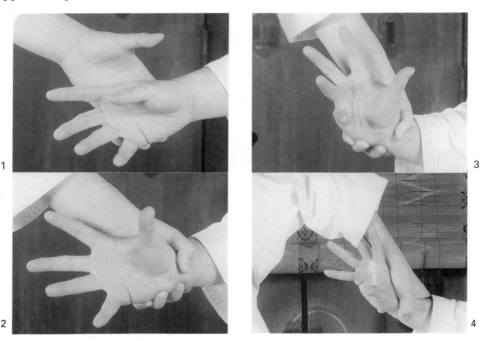

Aiki-age: When *uke* grabs *tori's* wrist, *tori* spreads his fingers so that his hand looks like a morning glory in full bloom. Keeping his thumb immobile, *tori* rotates his wrist and elbow upward, knocking *uke* off balance.

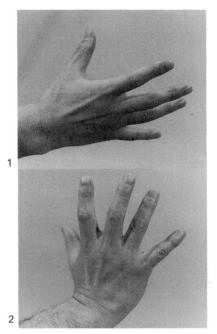
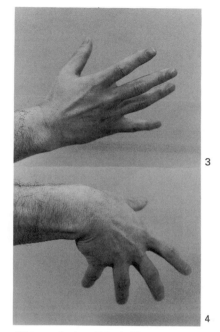

Aiki-age (using *fudō daiji*).   *Aiki-sage* (using *fudō shōji*).

A practical exercise based on these two principles is the "eight-direction-throw" (*happō*), also known as the "fire-dragon eight-direction throw" (*karyū happō*). Begin by placing yourself in the sitting position facing south—in the *I Ching* it states "Kings face the south," and Japanese shrines typically also face south—and have your standing opponent grab both hands:

1. The first throw (*karyū gonhō*) is diagonally to the northeast, location of the "demon-gate" where events originate, according to Japanese popular belief. This throw also symbolizes the dispersal of evil.
2. The second throw (*karyū kenhō*) is diagonally to the northwest.
3. The third throw (*karyū sonhō*) is diagonally to the southeast.
4. The fourth throw (*karyū konhō*) is diagonally to the southwest.
5. The fifth throw (*karyū kanhō*) is straight back to the north.
6. The sixth throw (*karyū rihō*) is straight to the south.
7. The seventh throw (*karyū shinhō*) is sideways to the east.
8. The eighth throw (*karyū dahō*) is sideways to the west.

This technique can alternatively be performed with both partners standing and conclude with a pin, but this variation is part of a separate set of *aiki* techniques.

Karyū happō

1. *Karyū gonhō.*

2. *Karyū kenhō.*

3. *Karyū sonhō.*

4. *Karyū konhō.*

Karyū happō

5. *Karyū kanhō.*

6. *Karyū rihō.*

7. *Karyū shinhō.*

8. *Karyū dahō.*

The Spirit of Aiki

IKI, the art of negating an opponent's strength, can be demonstrated in many different ways, with varying degrees of accuracy. However, total understanding of all its subtle dimensions is rare, since *aiki* has complex spiritual, physiological, and physical dimensions.

The spiritual dimension of *aiki* involves a number of factors: power of suggestion, psychology, and susceptibility. For example, it may be possible to execute a technique in a certain *dōjō* (training hall) because its practitioners are accustomed to that kind of training and are susceptible to the seeming effects of that technique—a kind of mass hypnosis. At another *dōjō* the same technique may be completely ineffective. It is undeniable that some people are more suggestible than others, and a charismatic instructor good at reading that sensitivity can perform feats that appear amazing, such as downing an attacker without touching the person, or remaining immobile even with several people shoving him. The relationship between the power of suggestion and true mental power in *aiki* is very complex, and it is not easy to differentiate between the two.

Good *aiki* technique is based on knowledge of how the body responds to certain movements and degrees of pressure. It is easy to see that relaxed shoulders and slightly bent arms generate more power than tight shoulders and stiffly extended arms, and that the economical use of physical power goes a long way. In another form of physiological *aiki*, *kaishō no den* (simply spreading the fingers widely when grabbed) makes it easier to control an attack. Yet another form is *atemi* (strikes). This kind of blow is delivered with the entire hand but is preceded by the touch of one finger. Because the opponent reacts unconsciously to the finger's touch, he then also feels the single, light blow of *atemi* throughout his body. This kind of *aiki atemi* is also one of the secret techniques of Chinese Kung-fu taught only to senior trainees, and it has also been employed by many traditional Japanese martial art systems.

Aiki includes a number of techniques that function on the pulley principle. A pul-

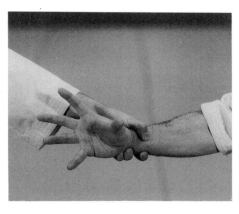

Kaishō no den
Spreading your fingers widely in response
when an opponent grabs your wrist.

ley can change both the direction and the amount of a force, using the principle of
zero resistance. With even a small revolution, a pulley can make it possible to move a
large object. Similarly, when an opponent grabs your wrist, you can move another
part of your arm (for instance, the elbow), so that rather than moving the wrist you
use it as a "fixed pulley" and present a strong counter to the attack. However, if the
opponent pushes, or pulls, or has a very strong grip, this principle does not work as
well. In such cases, a larger circular motion of the body, such as the *en no sabaki* circular movement (pivoting on one foot while making a big, sweeping turn) employed
in Ueshiba-style Aikido, can be quite effective. Again, the main principles are non-
resistance to and redirection of a force.

In practical terms, we use the techniques of *aiki-age* and *aiki-sage*. When an opponent holds your wrist, spread your fingers with a certain amount of force, but keep the
rest of your arm relaxed. If your entire arm is stiff you cannot react to sudden pushes
and pulls. In short, keep calm and relaxed and abandon all use of inefficient force.

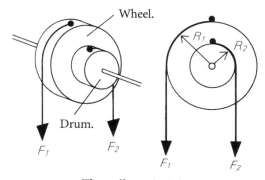

The pulley principle.

II

TECHNIQUES

Basic Techniques

Ikka-jō

Uke delivers a strike with his right hand to *tori*'s head. *Tori* rises up in the fire-dragon motion (*aiki-age*), blocks the attack, grabs *uke*'s arm at the wrist and elbow, and drives the arm back toward *uke*'s head. (In this last movement, called *fūkaku den*, each technique must emanate from a straight and centered line, similar to a plumb line in construction.) *Tori* advances first on his left knee and then slightly on his right knee to bring *uke* facedown to the ground. *Uke* is pinned at the elbow with the arm or, as is seen in the Variation, with the knee. Note that in the Variation *tori* has his right foot under *uke*'s hand.

1   2

3

4

5

Variation

1

2

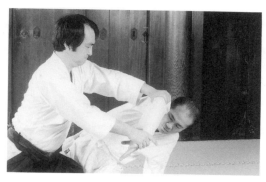

Fūkaku den

This involves bringing the opponent down by attacking his center. Grasp his arm at the elbow and push it (either bent at the elbow or straight) toward his ear or his nose.

Nika-jō

Uke grabs *tori's* collar. *Tori* delivers *atemi* to *uke's* face, raises himself onto his left knee (with his right leg at a right angle) and grabs *uke's* hand and wrist in the *nika-jō* lock as shown, applying pressure as if cutting down through *uke's* center, to bring *uke* to the ground (this last movement is another example of *fūkaku den*). The pin may alternatively be completed as in the Variation shown here.

5

7

6

Variation

Sanka-jō

Tori delivers a blow to *uke's* head, forcing *uke* to block it with his right hand. *Tori* grabs *uke's* fingers and pulls downward toward the mat. *Tori* then brings *uke's* arm back up in front of his own face, as if he were taking a sip from a glass (this movement is called *guinomi kuden.*) Next, *tori* switches hands so that he is holding *uke's* right hand in his own left hand, as lightly as if he were holding a fishing rod (*tsurizao kuden*, or "fishing pole" lock). *Tori* brings *uke* down to the ground and completes the pin, as in the original technique or the Variation shown.

5

6

7

8

9

10

Variation

Guinomi kuden: Grab your opponent's fingers as shown, and raise them as if you were taking a sip of saké.

Tsurizao kuden: When applying *sanka-jō*, hold your opponent's hand as shown, initiating the movement of a fishing pole at the moment in which a fish strikes the line. Be careful not to bend your opponent's arm at either the wrist or the elbow, since doing so would render the lock ineffective.

Yonka-jō

Uke grabs *tori's* right wrist with his right hand. *Tori* opens up slightly to his right, rotates *uke's* arm with his right hand, and grabs *uke's* wrist at the pulse with his left hand, and then applies *yonka-jō* while also executing the *kannuki kuden* "bolt" lock with the joint of his index finger. He steps forward onto his left knee and drives *uke* down to the ground. There is also an optional Variation for completing the pin.

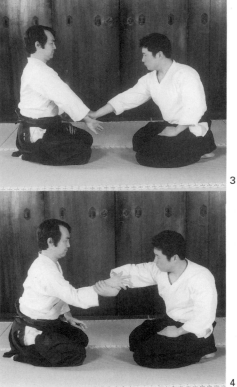

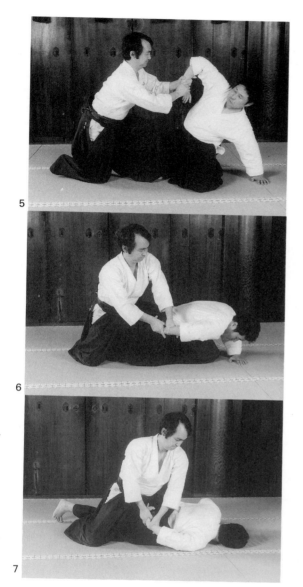

5

6

7

Kannuki kuden

Yonka-jō is best performed together with the *kannuki kuden* "bolt" lock, which involves keeping your arm straight, from the shoulder all the way to the tip of the index finger, and then directing all your force onto the base of your index finger.

Variation

Goka-jō

Uke delivers a punch with his right fist toward *tori's* solar plexus. *Tori* slides to the side, uses his left hand-sword to deflect the blow, and controls *uke's* wrist with the "fishhook" hold (*tsuribari kuden*). *Tori* then delivers *atemi* to *uke's* face, applies the *goka-jō* lock as shown, and then releases his right hand and brings *uke* down to the ground by cutting downward with his left hand. *Tori* raises *uke's* elbow with his left hand and pins *uke* as shown, with his left knee on *uke's* shoulder and his right knee on *uke's* hand.

5

7

6

Tsuribari kuden

Rather than tightly grabbing an opponent's wrist, it is often more effective to use your little finger and/or thumb to "hook" his hand as shown and apply the pin. This "fishhook" type of hold also works well with techniques other than *goka-jō*, and so is useful to always keep in mind.

Rokka-jō

Uke delivers a *yokomen* (blow to the side of the head) attack with his right hand. *Tori* receives the blow with his left hand and then shifts both hands to apply the *shihō-nage* grip. Sweeping his arm along in an arc shape as if he were scooping water out from the bottom of a rounded boat (in the movement known as *funazoko kuden*), *tori* spins *uke* in the opposite direction, and then brings him down to the mat with pressure to his head and arm, as shown. The concluding pin also has an optional Variation.

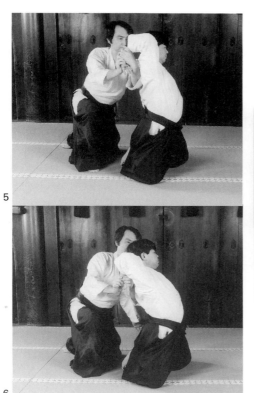

5

6

7

Variation

1

2

3

Irimi-nage

Uke attempts a *shōmen* blow to *tori's* head. *Tori* steps in with his left leg, receives the blow with his right hand-sword and then sweeps around to *uke's* right as shown. *Tori* raises his right hand and cradles *uke's* head in both his arms while pressing on the *dokko* pressure point on *uke's* neck (*dokko den*). *Tori* then steps forward on his right leg while bringing his right arm downward toward the ground to effect the throw.

Dokko den

In the execution of *irimi-nage* it is important to control your opponent's entire body, and not just his head and neck. Pressing on the *dokko* pressure point on the neck just below the ear weakens *uke's* entire body, which means that he can be controlled and thrown.

Shihō-nage

Uke attempts a *yokomen* strike to *tori's* head with his right hand. *Tori* slides forward on his left leg, then takes a wide step forward on his right leg. Then *tori* simultaneously blocks *uke's* attack and delivers a counter-blow to *uke's* neck, in the *aiki* two-sword style. Next, *tori* shifts his right hand to take hold of *uke's* pulse (*myaku-mochi no den*). *Tori* steps forward on his left leg, raises his hands as if lifting a sword heavenward, and, after planting his left foot, turns 180 degrees, keeping *uke's* arm in front of his own center while cutting downward toward the earth (*tenchi no den*) to effect the throw.

5

***Aiki* two-sword principle** (detail).

6

7

8

Tenchi no den (detail). Lit., "heaven/earth" movement. When you do *shihō-nage*, grasp your opponent's hand, with your index finger sticking straight up (toward "heaven"). Twist your opponent's wrist outward and conclude with your index finger pointing down (toward earth). Your *shihō-nage* technique can be made extremely effective if you also add *yonka-jō* at the same time.

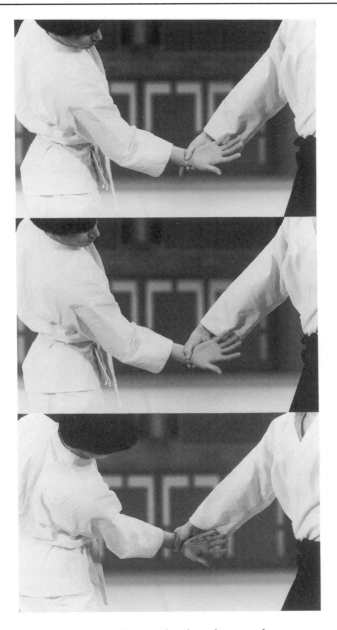

Myaku-mochi no den (detail). Use the thumb to apply pressure to your opponent's pulse. It is not effective, however, to immediately grasp the opponent's hand at the pulse area. The secret here instead is to grasp from the opposite side, with your thumb near the base of the little finger, and to slide it down to the pulse.

Kote-gaeshi

Uke thrusts toward *tori's* stomach with his right fist. *Tori* slides forward on his left leg, grips *uke's* arm lightly with both his hands, and applies pressure to *uke's* elbow with his hips. The hold on *uke's* hand is based on the "fishhook" principle, and *tori's* left thumb presses on the pressure point near *uke's* ring finger. *Tori* sweeps around with his right foot, delivering *atemi* to *uke's* back with his elbow. *Tori* then steps forward on his right leg, swivels his hips, and applies the *kote-gaeshi* lock, keeping his hands at approximately the level of his belt (*obigurai no den*). *Tori* cuts downward in front of his own center to bring *uke* to the ground, and completes the technique with a pin, as shown.

5

6

7

Tenchi-nage

Uke grabs both of *tori's* wrists. *Tori* steps forward with his left leg and immediately executes *aiki-age* with his right hand and *aiki-sage* with his left hand. *Tori* takes a wide step to the rear of *uke*, and brings both his hands together to complete the throw. If *uke's* grip is very strong and it is difficult to execute *aiki-age*, apply the "yin-yang" movement (*in'yō no den*). First turn the palm upward (yin) to neutralize *uke's* power, and then turn the palm downward (yang) while raising the arm, to guide *uke* in the proper direction.

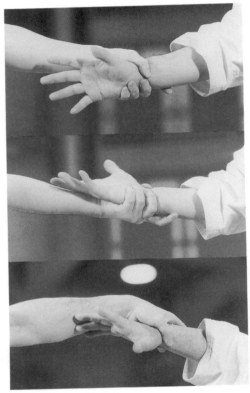

In'yō no den (detail).

When the opponent grasps your hand forcefully and you find that you are unable to do *aiki-age*, turn your hand first palm up, and then over so that the back faces up. This way, you can make your opponent's strength veer off course and free your own hand so that you can easily control the opponent.

Kaiten-nage

Uke grabs *tori's* left wrist with his right hand. *Tori* slides forward on his left leg and delivers *atemi* to *uke's* face with his right hand. *Tori* steps in with his right leg, turns 180 degrees, and then steps back on his left leg, changing his grip on *uke's* wrist. *Tori* guides *uke's* head down with a "feathery touch" (*umō no den*) with his right hand, then steps forward to complete the throw. In this and in several other techniques, a light, feathery touch is more effective than a rough, sudden pull.

Gyakuhiji-nage

Uke delivers a *yokomen* blow with his right hand-sword to *tori's* head. *Tori* moves in the same manner as in the *shihō-nage* techniques, first countering the attack in the *aiki* two-sword style, and then applying a "pulse hold" to *uke's* right wrist. *Tori* places his elbow under *uke's* elbow, keeping the palm of his hand facing upward. He then steps forward on his left foot to complete the throw and at that time turns his hand over so that the palm faces down (this movement of *tori's* hand is an example of *in'yō no den*).

Intermediate Techniques: Throwing

Ayate-dori kote-gaeshi

Uke grabs *tori*'s right wrist with his right hand. *Tori* steps forward on his left leg, applies the *kote-gaeshi* lock to *uke*'s wrist, slides both feet diagonally to *uke*'s right, and cuts downward on *uke*'s wrist to effect the throw.

2

1

3

4

5

Sode-tori aiki-nage

Uke grabs *tori*'s right elbow and wrist from behind and attempts to pin *tori*'s arm to his back. *Tori* rotates his hips 180 degrees to the right to face *uke*. *Tori* then raises his right arm in *aiki-age*, pushing against *uke*'s left wrist and controlling the left elbow, while sliding forward on his front leg to effect the throw.

Uke pins *tori*'s right arm against his back

Kata-dori oni no kubi

Uke grabs *tori*'s right shoulder with his left hand. *Tori* slides his right arm under *uke*'s arm and presses down on *uke*'s elbow joint in a circular motion with his right hand-sword. *Tori* turns his outstretched hand so that the palm is facing downward, brings his right hand-sword down into the crook of *uke*'s elbow, and then pulls his own arms in tightly to his sides. *Tori* holds *uke*'s hands firmly and twists, to bring *uke*'s head downward. *Tori* then places his right hand under *uke*'s chin, and left hand on the back of *uke*'s neck. Finally, *tori* presses down on *uke*'s head and twists his hips sharply to effect the throw.

1

2

3

4

5

7

6

8

9

10

Ryō-eri-dori mute-nage

Uke grabs *tori*'s collar and applies a choke hold with both hands. *Tori* delivers *atemi* to *uke*'s stomach with his right fist, pulls in his chin, and slides his head, from the left, in between *uke*'s arms. *Tori* then twists his hips and steps forward forcefully with his left leg, throwing *uke* straight ahead.

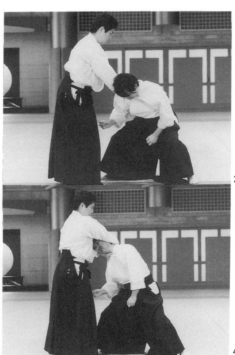

Shōmen-uke aiki-nage (omote)

Uke delivers a *shōmen* strike to *tori*'s head with his right hand-sword. *Tori* advances quickly and blocks the attack before *uke* has a chance to complete the strike. *Tori* then slides forward on his front foot and redirects the attack toward *uke*, causing *uke* to fall backward.

5

6

7

8

Shōmen-uke aiki-nage (ura)

Uke delivers a *shōmen* strike to *tori*'s head with his right hand-sword. *Tori* steps out on his left foot to *uke*'s right, avoiding the attack, and while turning his hips uses his right hand to apply the "fishhook" hold (*tsuribari kuden*) on *uke*'s arm, just before throwing *uke* with a large, sweeping motion.

1   2

3

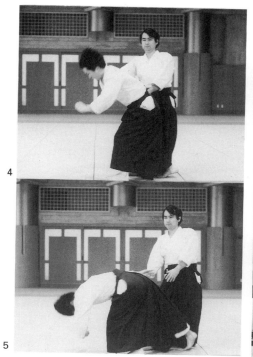

4

5

6

7

8

Yokomen-uke aiki-nage (omote)

Uke delivers a *yokomen* strike to the side of *tori*'s head with his right hand-sword. *Tori* slides in diagonally and uses his left hand-sword to stop and redirect the attacking force to *uke*'s rear. *Tori* continues to slide in, while cutting downward, to effect the throw.

5

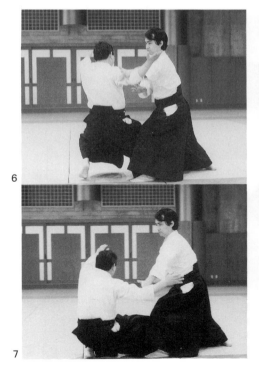

6

7

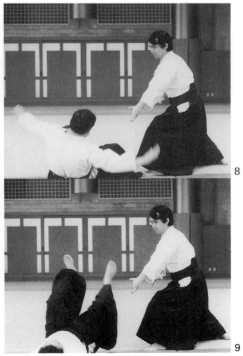

8

9

Yokomen-uke aiki-nage (ura)

Uke delivers a *yokomen* strike to *tori*'s head with his right hand-sword. *Tori* steps out on his right leg and employs the "fishhook" hold with his left hand to cut down on *uke*'s attacking arm and throw *uke* straight ahead.

4

6

5

7

8

Tsuki-uke ryū no agito

Uke delivers a thrust to *tori*'s stomach with his right fist. *Tori* slides forward on his front leg to avoid the attack and rotates his right arm counterclockwise beneath *uke*'s right arm. *Tori* then thrusts toward *uke*'s chin with his right hand, takes a wide step in with his right leg, and pushes downward to effect the throw.

5

6

7

8

9

Tsuki-uke gyakuhiji-nage

Uke delivers a punch to *tori*'s stomach with his right fist. *Tori* slides forward on his front foot to avoid the attack, catches *uke*'s arm, and positions his left elbow under *uke*'s elbow. *Tori* sweeps around with his right leg and pushes down on *uke*'s arm to effect the throw.

5

7

6

8

9

Tsuki-uke oguruma-nage

Uke delivers a thrust to *tori*'s stomach with his right fist. *Tori* slides back slightly to avoid the attack and grabs *uke*'s attacking arm slightly above the wrist. *Tori* raises *uke*'s arm, slides his right hand between the elbow and wrist in the *oguruma* lock, then takes a step in with his right leg and cuts downward with his hands to effect the throw.

5

6

7

8

9

10

Konoha-otoshi (yō)

Uke delivers a strike toward *tori*'s neck with his right hand-sword. *Tori* pivots to the inside of the attacking arm and rotates his right hand-sword counterclockwise around *uke*'s wrist. While continuing to turn in, *tori* grabs *uke*'s right wrist and cuts downward to effect the throw.

4

5

6

7

Konoha-otoshi (in)

Uke attempts to grab *tori*'s right hand with his own right hand. *Tori* immediately spreads his fingers and places his right palm against *uke*'s right palm, directing the attacking force up and then downward. *Tori* then takes a step forward with his right leg to effect the throw.

5

6

7

8

9

Intermediate Techniques: Pinning

THE PINNING techniques shown here are a representative sample of beginning, intermediate, and advanced techniques. Many of these techniques can also be executed as throws.

Ryō-eri-dori ryū no agito

Uke grabs *tori*'s collar with both hands and applies a choke hold. *Tori* uses his left hand-sword to counter the choke hold by pushing *uke*'s left elbow to the side, and then thrusts the heel of his right palm against *uke*'s chin. *Tori* slides forward on his front leg and pushes *uke* back with a straight arm to the chin.

1   2

3

5

4

6

7

Karami-shibori

Uke grabs *tori*'s right wrist with his right hand and applies a choke hold to *tori*'s neck from behind with his left hand. *Tori* raises his right hand in *aiki-age* over his head, applies a *sanka-jō* lock to *uke*'s right hand, and cuts downward, pinning *uke*'s arms in a cross.

Sode-tori kukuri

Uke grabs *tori*'s left sleeve with his right hand. *Tori* raises his left arm in *aiki-age* and steps to *uke*'s right side and turns, rotating his left hand-sword under *uke*'s elbow. *Uke* is forced to turn, and *tori* positions himself behind *uke*'s back. *Tori* grabs *uke*'s right hand and pins it under his chin, immobilizing *uke* as shown.

Sode-tori makihiji

Uke grabs *tori*'s left sleeve with his right hand. *Tori* raises his arm in *aiki-age* and rotates his left hand-sword counterclockwise under *uke*'s right elbow. *Tori* raises his hand-sword under *uke*'s elbow, knocking him off balance, then pins *uke*'s right arm tightly against his body.

Sode-tori nika-jō-gatame

Uke grabs *tori*'s right sleeve with his left hand. *Tori* rotates his right hand-sword counterclockwise to the outside of *uke*'s wrist, and breaks *uke*'s posture. *Tori* rotates his right hand-sword under *uke*'s elbow, and applies the *nika-jō* pin.

4

5

6

Karami-gatame

Uke grabs *tori*'s right shoulder with his left hand and delivers a *shōmen* strike to the head with his right hand. *Tori* blocks the strike with his right hand-sword and then cuts down and grabs *uke*'s right hand. *Tori* grabs *uke*'s left hand just above the wrist and twists. *Tori* then grabs *uke*'s right wrist, swivels his hips, applies a cross-lock to *uke*'s arms and brings him to the ground, completing the pin as shown.

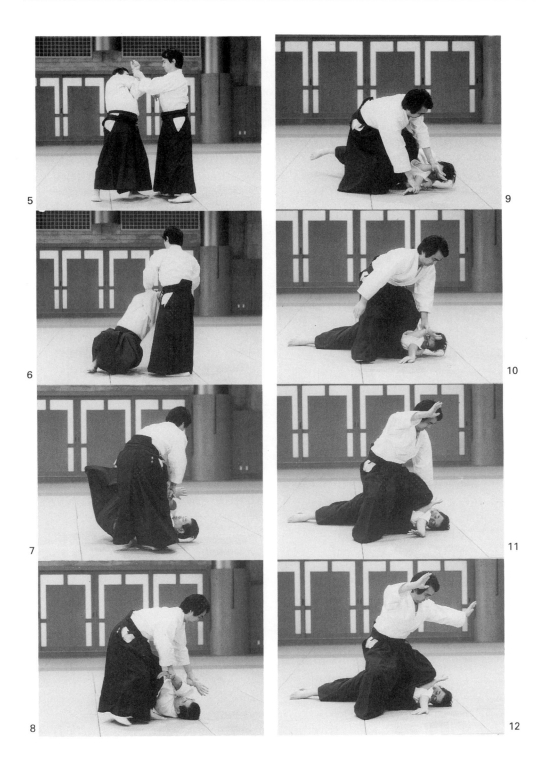

Fūrai

Uke grabs *tori*'s right hand with his own left hand. *Tori* immediately applies the *yonka-jō* lock to *uke*'s left wrist, then cuts down to bring *uke* to the ground. *Tori* concludes the pin by placing his left foot on *uke*'s neck and switching hands to pin *uke*'s left arm.

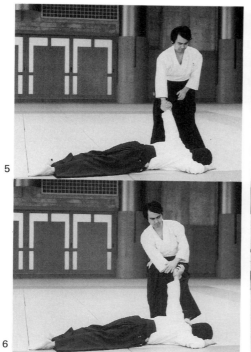

Ushiro-dori hitoe

Uke grabs *tori*'s wrists from behind. *Tori* twists his hips to the right, holds *uke*'s left hand against his hip, and raises his right arm in *aiki-age*. *Tori* takes a large step back on his right leg, grabs *uke*'s right wrist, and brings *uke*'s arm back over *uke*'s head. *Uke* is pinned over *tori*'s right leg, and the technique is completed with an *atemi* to *uke*'s solar plexus.

4

5

6

7

Ayate-dori tenbin

Uke grabs *tori*'s right wrist with his right hand. *Tori* steps diagonally to the right and then forward with his left leg, while raising *uke*'s wrist and placing his shoulder under *uke*'s elbow. *Tori* cuts down with his right hand and raises his shoulder to immobilize *uke*.

4

5

6

Ushiro-dori gyakuhiji-gatame

Uke grabs *tori*'s wrists from behind. *Tori* turns his hips to the right, raises his hands in *aiki-age*, slips under *uke*'s arms, and grabs *uke*'s left elbow with his right hand. *Tori* cuts down forcefully on *uke*'s right elbow with his right hand-sword and applies *nika-jō* to *uke*'s right wrist with his left hand. *Tori* slides forward on his front foot and presses down on *uke*'s arm to complete the pin.

5

6

7

8

9

10

Futae ude-makura

Uke tries to grab *tori*'s wrists. But before he can, *tori* grabs the backs of *uke*'s hands and steps directly behind *uke*, bringing his arms up and back. *Tori* pins *uke*'s head against *tori*'s own left knee. *Tori* then pulls *uke*'s elbows down against him and releases his grip, stretching his arms out to either side.

5

6

7

8

9

10

Hangetsu-kuzushi

Uke attempts to grab *tori*'s wrists. But before he can, *tori* grabs *uke*'s left wrist with his left hand and *uke*'s right wrist from above with his right hand. *Tori* then steps in with his left leg and turns 180 degrees. *Tori* extends his right arm fully and pins *uke*'s left arm under his chin.

4

5

6

7

8

Toami

Uke delivers a *shōmen* strike to *tori*'s head with his right hand-sword. *Tori* steps in with his right leg, crosses his arms, and blocks the attack. *Tori* then cuts downward with his left hand-sword and grabs *uke*'s wrist at the pulse with his right hand. Next, *tori* steps in with his left leg, pivots 180 degrees, and cuts downward to bring *uke* to the ground. *Tori* then grabs *uke*'s right wrist with both hands, and applies pressure to *uke*'s wrist and elbow to complete the pin.

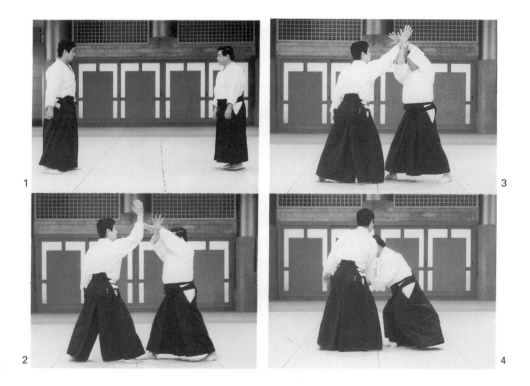

5

6

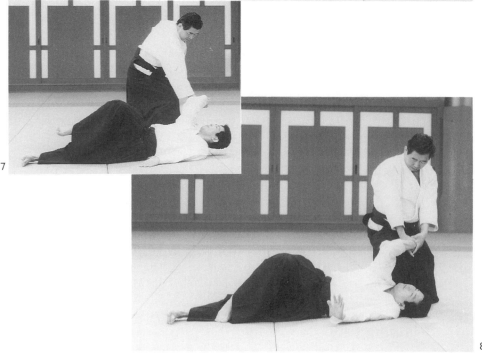

7

8

Kusanagi

Uke delivers a *yokomen* strike to *tori*'s neck. *Tori* steps out with his right leg and blocks the strike with his left hand-sword while applying *atemi* to *uke*'s neck. *Tori* then grabs *uke*'s right wrist at the pulse with his right hand, steps in with his left leg, and pivots 180 degrees. *Tori* grabs *uke*'s right wrist with both hands, and then pulls *uke*'s wrist straight down to bring *uke* to the ground. *Tori* then applies pressure with his big toe to the pressure point inside *uke*'s knee, and completes the pin by pulling up on *uke*'s right hand.

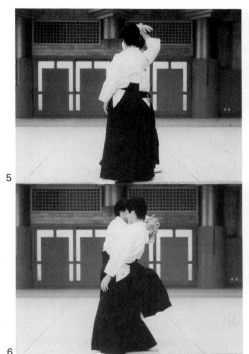

5

7

6

8

9

10

Taizan

Uke grabs *tori*'s left collar with his right hand. *Tori* grabs *uke*'s right wrist at the pulse with his right hand, slides out to the left with his front foot, and then pivots clockwise 180 degrees. *Tori* then cuts down in front of his own center to bring *uke* to the ground and presses down on *uke*'s right side with his knee. He then places his left knee on *uke*'s right elbow and his right knee on *uke*'s trunk. When the pin is completed, he releases both his hands.

Kairi

Uke delivers a punch to *tori*'s stomach with his right fist. *Tori* moves around to *uke*'s right side, applies a *kote-gaeshi* hold on *uke*'s right wrist, and then pivots 180 degrees. *Tori* grabs *uke*'s left forearm and pulls it forward. Holding both of *uke*'s wrists, *tori* drops to the ground, bringing *uke* with him. *Tori* completes the pin by holding *uke*'s arms between his knees.

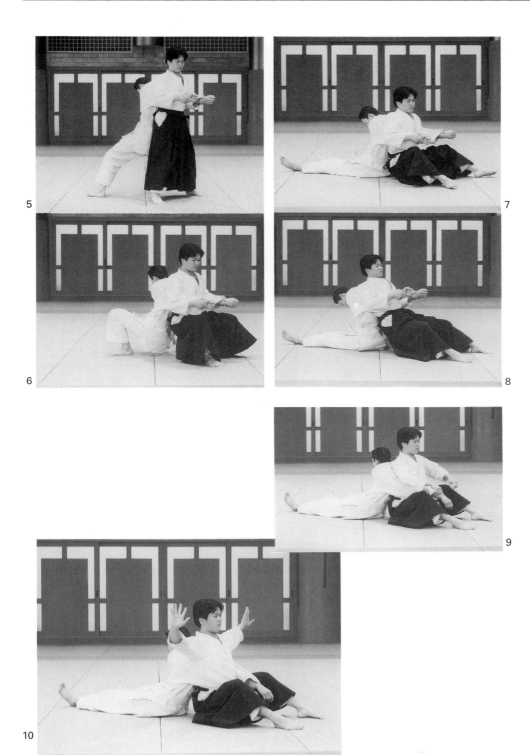

5

6

7

8

9

10

Kamakubi-gatame

Uke delivers a *shōmen* strike with his right hand-sword. *Tori* steps out on his left leg and blocks *uke*'s attack with both hands. *Tori* then grabs *uke*'s wrist with his right hand and *uke*'s elbows with his left hand, moves around to *uke*'s right side, and rotates *uke*'s arm down to chest level. Next, *tori* takes hold of *uke*'s right hand from underneath with his left hand and pins *uke*'s elbow against his chest to complete the technique.

5

6

7

8

Kaede-awase

Uke grabs *tori*'s right wrist with his right hand. *Tori* applies *aiki-age* and cuts downward, bringing *uke* to the ground. *Tori* rotates his right hand, positioning it palm-to-palm with *uke*'s hand, and then presses down and a bit forward on *uke*'s arm to effect the pin.

Hachiwari

Standing diagonally to *tori*'s right, *uke* delivers a strike to the head with his right hand-sword. *Tori* slides in diagonally with his right foot, grabs *uke*'s wrist with his right hand and *uke*'s elbow with his left hand, and pushes *uke* back and down. *Tori* then slides his left arm under *uke*'s right arm and delivers *atemi* to *uke*'s neck with his right hand-sword. Next, *tori* presses firmly down on *uke*'s neck with his right hand and slides his left arm in to pin both of *uke*'s arms, as shown.

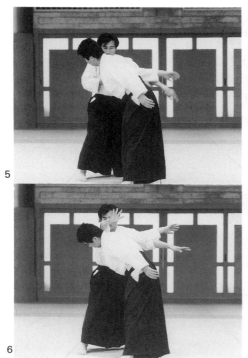

5

7

6

8

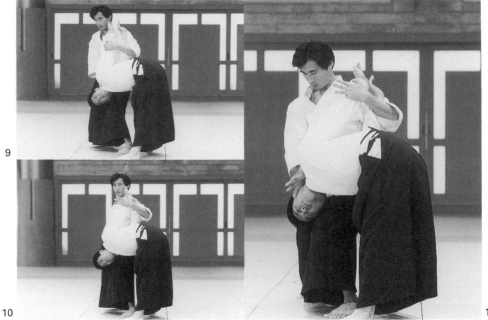

9

10

11

Yumi

Uke delivers a punch to *tori*'s stomach with his right fist. *Tori* steps out with his left leg, grabs *uke*'s right wrist at the pulse with his right hand, and pushes against *uke*'s chin with his left hand-sword. *Tori* then pulls on *uke*'s right arm while pushing against his neck to stretch *uke* out in an arc shape. *Tori* may also wrap his arm around *uke*'s neck and apply a choke hold.

5

6

7

Hashira-tate

Uke grabs *tori*'s right wrist with his left hand. *Tori* applies *aiki-age* with his right hand and then steps back, bringing *uke* facedown to the ground. Then *tori* rotates his right hand-sword until that hand is palm-to-palm with *uke*'s left hand. Next, *tori* swings his right leg around *uke*'s upraised arm, places his foot between *uke*'s neck and shoulder, and applies pressure with his right knee to complete the pin.

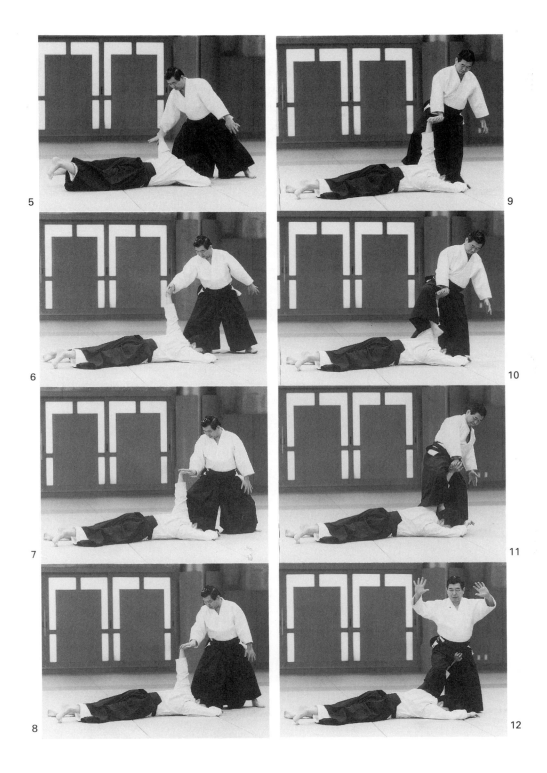

Tsutakazura

Uke delivers a kick to *tori*'s stomach with his right leg. *Tori* steps out on his right leg to *uke*'s right side and catches the attacking leg from below with a counterclockwise motion of his right hand-sword. *Tori* then pins *uke*'s leg against his right shoulder, holds *uke*'s right elbow with his left hand, and takes a large step in with his right leg to bring *uke* down to the ground. *Tori* swings his left leg in over *uke*'s right leg, plants his foot firmly on the ground, and uses his arms to twist *uke*'s leg in the opposite direction to effect the pin.

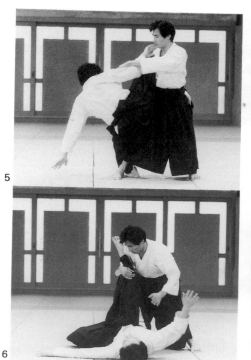

5

7

6

8

9

10

Kusabi-omoshi

Uke grabs *tori*'s left wrist with his right hand. *Tori* slides forward on his front foot while delivering *atemi* to *uke*'s face, and rotates his left hand to apply a *nika-jō* lock to *uke*'s right wrist. *Tori* then brings *uke* facedown to the ground, pins *uke*'s right arm with his left knee, and completes the pin by sitting on *uke*'s back.

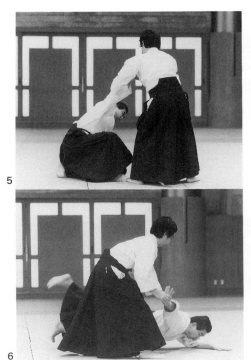

5

7

6

8

9

10

11

Fukuto

Uke grabs *tori*'s wrists. *Tori* raises both arms in *aiki-age* and then suddenly thrusts them apart, forcing *uke*'s head down. *Tori* then pins *uke*'s head between his knees and pulls *uke*'s arms up to effect the pin.

Ura-ageha

Uke grabs *tori*'s left wrist with his right hand. *Uke* applies a *nika-jō* lock to *uke*'s right hand. When *uke* loosens his grip on *tori*'s right wrist, *tori* pulls *uke*'s right hand downward while also twisting it outward. *Tori* places his left arm under *uke*'s right shoulder and *uke*'s right arm over his own left hand, then applies a *nika-jō* lock. *Tori* then presses his right leg against *uke*'s head. He catches *uke*'s right hand with his own right hand. *Tori* stands in front of *uke*, facing in the same direction, and reaches behind him to catch up *uke*'s arms in the crooks of his own arms, and draws *uke*'s arms forward to effect the pin.

Jōto

Uke grabs *tori*'s wrists. *Tori* raises both arms in *aiki-age*, then suddenly first spreads his arms wide and cuts downward with them, forcing *uke*'s head all the way to the ground. *Tori* grabs both of *uke*'s palms and pulls back. To complete the pin, *tori* swings his right leg around *uke*'s arms and sits down on *uke*'s back.

1

2

3

4

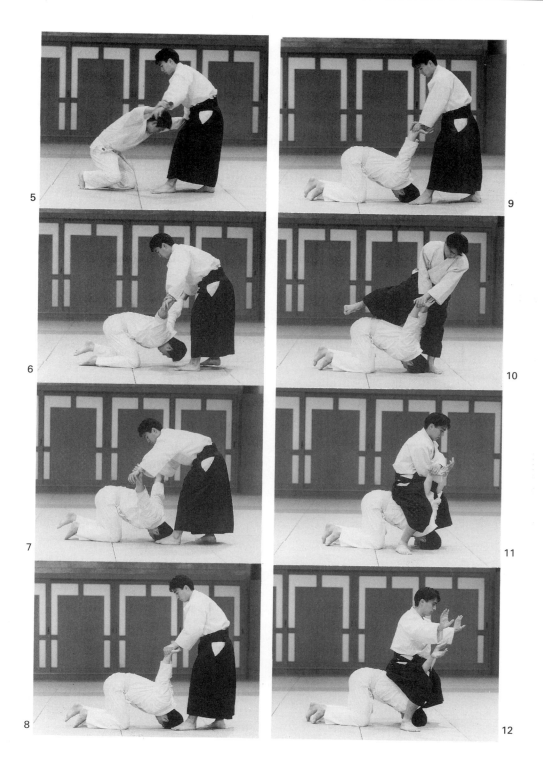

Ashibune

Uke delivers a *yokomen* strike to *tori*'s neck. *Tori* slides in with his front foot and absorbs *uke*'s attack with his left hand-sword, then cuts down with his right hand-sword, taking hold of *uke*'s right wrist. *Tori* steps in front of *uke* with his right leg, wraps *uke*'s right arm around *uke*'s neck, and with his left hand grabs *uke*'s wrist to create a choke hold. Next, *tori* twists his hips, bringing *uke* to the ground. *Tori* then turns *uke* facedown, wraps *uke*'s arms around *uke*'s neck, and pulls backward to complete the pin.

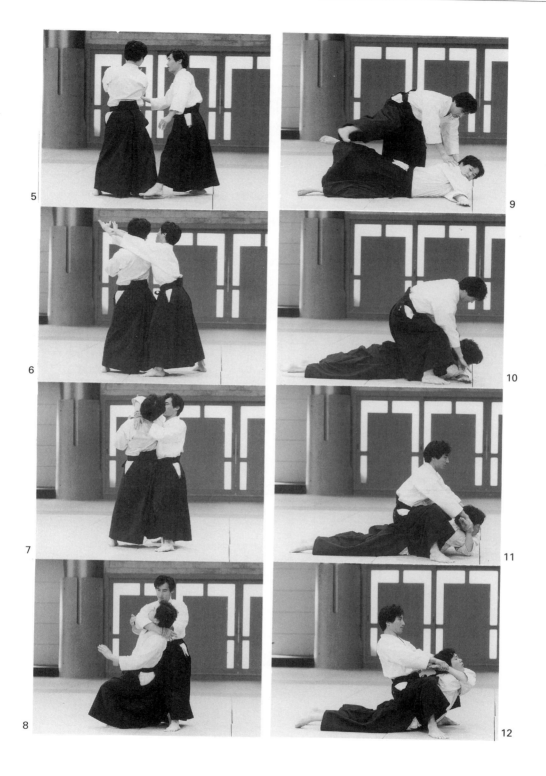

Hokuto

Uke grabs *tori*'s collar with his right hand. *Tori* takes hold of *uke*'s hand at the little-finger side with his own right hand, twists his hips sharply to the front, and applies a *nika-jō* lock. *Uke* drops to his knees and places his left hand on the ground. *Tori* then steps on *uke*'s left hand with his right foot, switches hands, places his right knee against *uke*'s side, and pulls up on *uke*'s right arm to effect the pin.

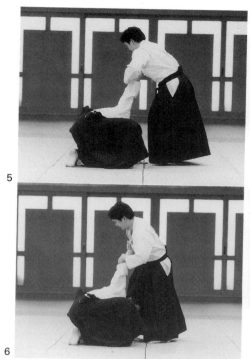

5

7

6

8

9

Fuji

Uke delivers a *shōmen* strike with his right hand-sword. *Tori* raises his arms in *aiki-age* and applies the *fūkaku* principle—blocking *uke*'s attacking arm at the wrist and elbow while taking a big step in with his front leg and cutting straight downward. *Tori* then secures *uke*'s right arm against his right knee, grabs *uke*'s left arm with his left hand and pulls it over *uke*'s head, and finally applies pressure with his right hand-sword to effect the pin.

Ukifune

Uke delivers a punch to *tori*'s stomach with his right fist. *Tori* steps out on his left leg while hitting *uke*'s wrist with his right hand-sword and *uke*'s elbow with his left hand-sword. With his left hand, he takes hold of *uke*'s right wrist. *Tori* sweeps his right leg around to the back and applies *atemi* with his right elbow to *uke*'s back. *Tori* brings his right leg back to its original position and with the back of his right fist hits *uke* in the face. He then drags the fist down to the inside of *uke*'s elbow, to bring *uke* down. He applies *atemi* to *uke*'s right elbow with his right sword-hand. *Uke* is now facedown, and *tori* pulls *uke*'s right hand up behind *uke*'s back, and then as far as *uke*'s shoulder. To complete the pin, he puts his right knee on *uke*'s back, while grabbing *uke*'s right ankle with his left hand and *uke*'s left wrist with his right hand.

Advanced Techniques: Multiple Attackers

Futari-dori (1)

Uke 1 grips *tori*'s left hand from the left with his left hand and *uke* 2 grips *tori*'s right hand with his right hand. *Tori* raises his right hand-sword with *aiki-age* while stepping forward with his right leg. *Tori* grips the right hands of both *uke*, turns, and pulls their hands behind his head. He moves *uke* 1 over to the left. He crosses the arms of the two *uke*, one over the other, and brings both *uke* to the ground. *Tori* pins one arm of each *uke* with his right knee to complete the pin.

1

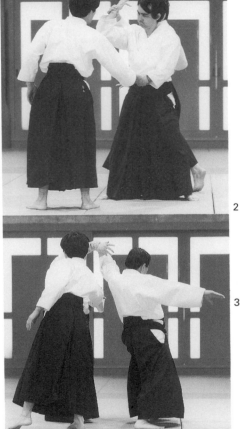

2

3

4

5

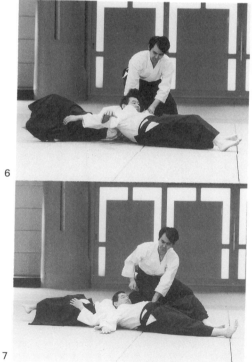

6

7

8

Futari-dori (2)

Uke 1 grabs *tori*'s left hand with both his hands while *uke* 2 grabs *tori*'s right hand with both hands. *Tori* grabs the right wrist of each *uke*, puts his left leg out diagonally, and then pivots 180 degrees to the right. *Tori* crosses the arms of the *uke*, one over the other, and pulls both *uke* to the ground, then pins their arms with his right knee to complete the technique.

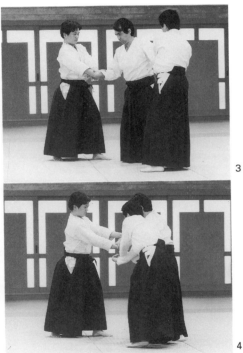

5

6

7

8

9

10

Futari-dori (3)

Uke 1 comes in from the left and grips *tori*'s left hand with his right hand. *Uke* 2 comes in from the right and takes *tori*'s right wrist with his left hand. *Tori* raises his arms in *aiki-age* and then sweeps down, after which he pulls his arms up again and twists them backward clockwise to release the grips of both *uke*. *Tori* catches one of the arms of *uke* 1 below his own and pins it down with his elbow, then catches the arm of *uke* 2 under the arm of *uke* 1 and pins it as well, bringing both *uke* to the ground. *Tori* then effects the pin by taking the free arm of each *uke* and crossing them over his own stomach and holding them in place at his hipbones, leaving his hands free.

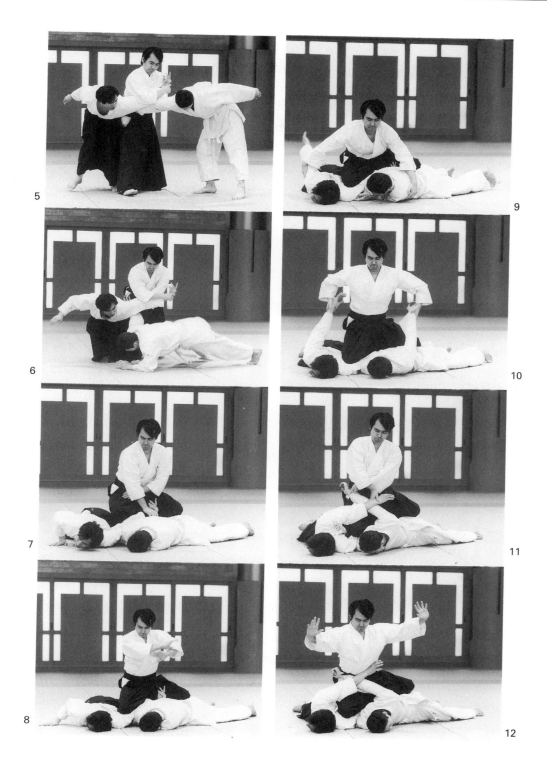

Sannin-dori

Uke 1 grabs *tori*'s right arm, *uke* 2 grabs *tori*'s left arm, and *uke* 3 grabs *tori*'s collar. *Tori* raises both arms in *aiki-age*, applies the *yonka-jō* lock to the two *uke* holding his arms, and turns *uke* 1 to the right by raising that *uke*'s right arm over his head. *Tori* crosses all of their arms together and cuts downward diagonally to bring all three to the ground. *Tori* then pins their arms with his right knee to complete the technique.

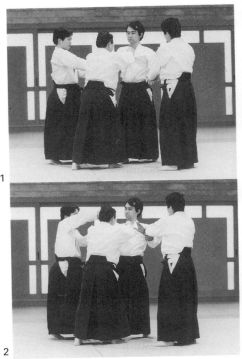

5

6

7

8

Yonin-dori

Four *uke* hold *tori* by both arms, and by his front and back collars. *Tori* raises both arms as if he was raising a pair of swords. *Tori* then steps forward on his right leg, twists his hips, and takes a sweeping step with his left leg, knocking the *uke* behind him to the ground. *Tori* pins the fallen *uke*'s arm with his right arm and continues to twist his hips, bringing the other three *uke* to the ground on top of the fallen *uke*.

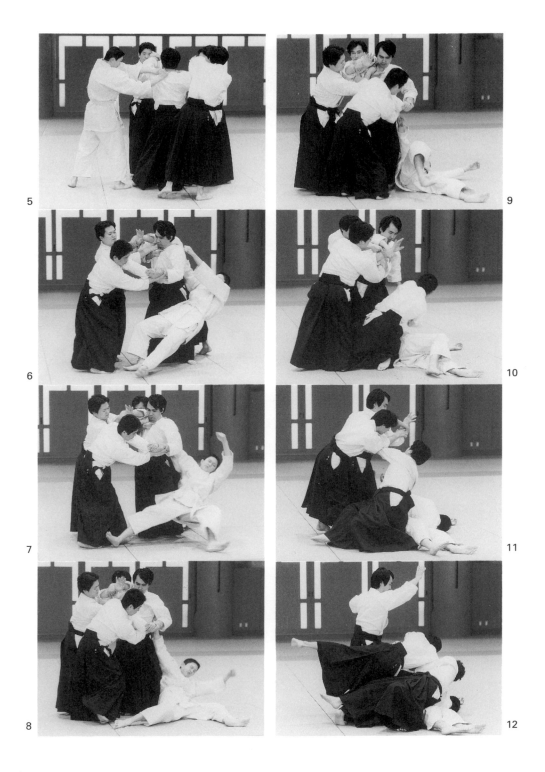

Gonin-dori

Five *uke* pin *tori* to the ground by his four limbs and his collar. *Tori* turns his knees inward, to pin the wrists of the two *uke* holding his ankles in *nika-jō* locks, while raising his head and applying *nika-jō* to the wrists of the two *uke* holding his arms, and then crossing the arms of those *uke* one over the other beneath the arms of the *uke* who is grasping his collar. *Tori* then slides out from the pin.

4

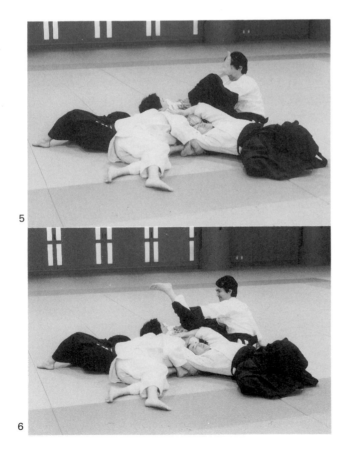

5

6

Advanced Techniques: Kaeshi-waza

KAESHI-WAZA are "reversal techniques" employed to counter an attempted throw or pin. Even without actually learning *kaeshi-waza*, most practitioners can sense when an opponent is being sloppy in a technique, making it easy to escape. Beginners are sometimes tempted to concentrate only on *kaeshi-waza*, imagining that such techniques will enable them to free themselves from any hold or pin. However, placing too great an emphasis on *kaeshi-waza* can actually impede learners' progress. Instead, the following advice should be borne in mind: "Since any technique can be countered with a *kaeshi-waza*, each technique must be executed with full concentration and careful attention to the smallest details." In fact, key to the proper execution of any technique is the principle of "never being careless."

Countering Ikka-jō with Aiki-nage

Two *uke* attempt to apply an *ikka-jo* pin to *tori*'s arms. *Tori* greatly lowers his hips to counter the attempted pin, raises his arms in *aiki-age*, takes a wide step with his right leg, and throws both *uke* to the rear.

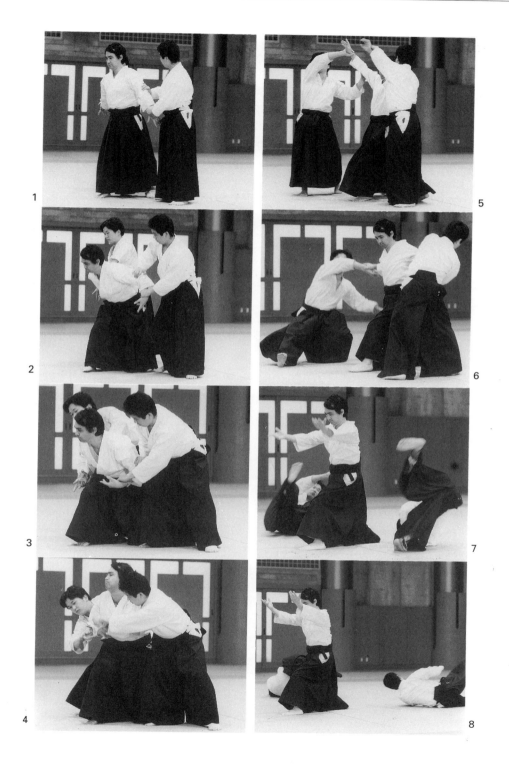

Countering Kote-gaeshi with Ikka-jō

Tori delivers a punch to *uke*'s stomach with his right fist. *Uke* steps in on his left leg and grips *tori*'s right wrist with his left hand. *Tori* slides his right leg back and brings his right elbow into *uke*'s back. *Uke* brings his legs back to their original position and, while gripping *tori*'s wrist, lays his right arm along *tori*'s left arm. He attempts to tourn *tori*'s wrist inward and pull him down, but *tori* makes his right hand lightly into a fist and rotates his fist around to the right (this motion is called the *neko no te kuden* or "cat's paw" movement). *Tori* then places his right elbow above *uke*'s left elbow, and aligns his left hand against *uke*'s left wrist. He then pins *uke*'s elbow.

Neko no te kuden

This motion is often used with *kaeshi-waza*. *Neko no te kuden* is a movement performed when an opponent is gripping your wrist. If, in response, you lightly make a fist, this will allow your hand to move in any direction and will make it easier to perform *kaeshi-waza*. This movement is also effective when applying *aiki* in a technique.

Countering Irimi-nage with Shihō-nage

Tori delivers a *shōmen* strike with his right hand-sword. *Uke* steps in with his left foot and attempts to perform the *irimi-nage* (entering throw) technique. *Tori* follows the flow of *uke*'s right hand, ducks his head, grabs *uke*'s right wrist with both his hands, steps in with his left leg, turns 180 degrees, and performs the *shihō-nage* (four-direction throw) technique.

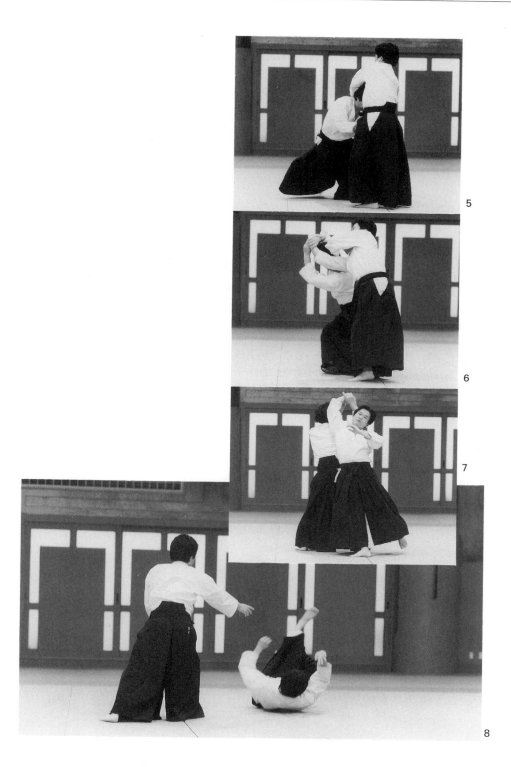

5

6

7

8

Countering Shihō-nage with Ikka-jō

Tori falls first, of his own accord, and spins out of the attempted pin. He hooks the middle finger and ring finger of his right hand around the edge of *uke*'s right hand (in the movement known as *nonaka no maku kuden*) and pulls *uke* down. *Tori* rises upon his right knee, and rests *uke*'s right wrist on that knee, while pressing on *uke*'s right elbow with his left hand. The pin is completed with a twist of *uke*'s wrist.

7

Nonaka no maku kuden

This motion takes its name from the kind of simple enclosure that might have surrounded a warrior's temporary encampment in an open field—composed of a frame of four strings held taut by four wooden stakes. *Nonaka no maku* conveys the idea that if a single string is touched, all the strings will hum; the phrase is used to refer to a motion that makes good use of the contact established between oneself and any point on the opponent's body. For instance, grabbing the opponent's sleeve and using it to throw him would fall into the category of *nonaka no maku*.

Countering Irimi-nage with Ashi-sarai

Tori delivers a *shōmen* strike with his right hand-sword. *Uke* moves to *tori*'s right, and blocks *tori*'s right hand-sword with his own right hand-sword. *Uke* then steps out onto his left leg. *Uke* pulls *tori*'s head to *uke*'s chest and draws his right leg backward and to the left, and brings down his right hand-sword, weakening *tori*'s power. *Uke* brings his right leg to the left of and behind *tori*, and at the same time turns his hand over so that it is facing downward, and sweeps it down, attempting to throw *tori*. *Tori* anticipates this move and falls before *uke* can throw him; at the same time, *tori* sweeps his right hand-sword along beneath *uke*'s left leg (which is bent at the knee). When *uke* falls, facedown, *tori* uses his right hand to grab the first and second toes of *uke*'s right foot, and then uses them to pull the foot toward *uke*'s back.

1

2

3

4

5

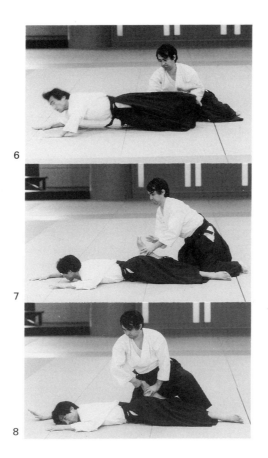

6

7

8

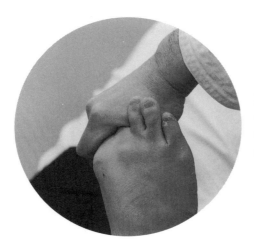

Detail of foot pin: Grab the opponent's big toe and first toe and bend them back toward the sole of the foot.

Other Techniques

THERE ARE FOUR WAYS to pin an attacker: pressing against the bones, twisting the muscles and joints, pinching the skin, and grabbing the hair. Attacks directed toward the skin and hair can be countered comparatively easily, and thus the techniques for dealing with such attacks have traditionally been kept secret in the Daitoryu. However, this section will introduce several such techniques, and conclude with instructions for dealing with an *uke* who is armed with a sword or with a *jō* (four-foot staff).

Kami no ke-dori ikka-jō

Uke grabs *tori*'s hair from behind with his right hand. *Tori* grabs *uke*'s hand with both his hands, turns in to the right, and applies pressure to *uke*'s wrist, causing him to float on his toes. *Tori* immediately cuts down with his hands, then presses down on *uke*'s elbow with his left hand to bring him to the ground. Next, *tori* pins *uke*'s shoulder and wrist, as shown.

Kami no ke-dori shihō-nage

Uke grabs *tori*'s hair from behind with his right hand. *Tori* grabs *uke*'s hand with both his hands, turns to the left, and applies pressure to *uke*'s wrist, causing him to float on his toes. *Tori* then turns to the right, steps in with his left leg, spins 180 degrees, and applies the *shihō-nage* technique.

5

6

7

8

Kami no ke-dori sanka-jō-kiritaoshi

Uke grabs *tori*'s hair from behind with his right hand. *Tori* grabs *uke*'s hand with both his hands, turns in to the right and applies pressure to *uke*'s wrist, causing him to float on his toes. *Tori* then takes a large step back and cuts down on *uke*'s wrist and elbow, bringing *uke* to the ground.

5

6

7

8

Tachi-dori aiki-nage

Uke delivers a *shōmen* cut with a sword. *Tori* steps in, delivers *atemi* to *uke*'s ribs, then turns in 180 degrees and grabs the hilt of *uke*'s sword. *Tori* then raises his right arm in *aiki-age* and throws *uke* straight ahead while maintaining his hold on the sword.

5

6

7

8

Tachi-dori kote-gaeshi

Uke delivers a *shōmen* cut with a sword. *Tori* steps in, delivers *atemi* to *uke*'s ribs, and applies the *kote-gaeshi* lock to *uke*'s right wrist. *Tori* then twists his hips, steps in with his right leg, and performs a *kote-gaeshi* throw. After bringing *uke* to the ground, *tori* disarms him and holds him at bay.

5

7

6

8

9

10

Tachi-dori shihō-nage

Uke delivers a *kesa-giri* (diagonal strike across the body) cut with a sword. *Tori* steps in with his right leg and delivers *atemi* to *uke*'s neck with his right hand while taking hold of the sword's grip with his left. *Tori* then steps in with his left leg and applies *shihō-nage*, being careful to keep the sword centered directly in front of him. While executing the throw, *tori* disarms *uke* and then holds him at bay.

1

2

3

4

5

6

7

8

9

10

11

Tachi-dori ikka-jō

Uke grabs *tori*'s right wrist with his right hand, attempting to prevent *tori* from drawing his sword. *Tori* grabs *uke*'s wrist with his right hand, twists his hip slightly to the right, and drives *uke*'s arm upward with his right hand while applying *atemi* to *uke*'s ribs with the sword pommel. *Tori* then pins *uke*'s elbow with the sword grip and brings him to the ground.

5

6

7

8

Tachi-dori nika-jō

With his right hand, *uke* grabs *tori*'s right wrist, attempting to prevent *tori* from drawing his sword. *Tori* twists his hips slightly to the right and raises the sword above *uke*'s wrist, then applies the *nika-jō* lock to *uke*'s wrist, using his hands and the sword grip to apply pressure.

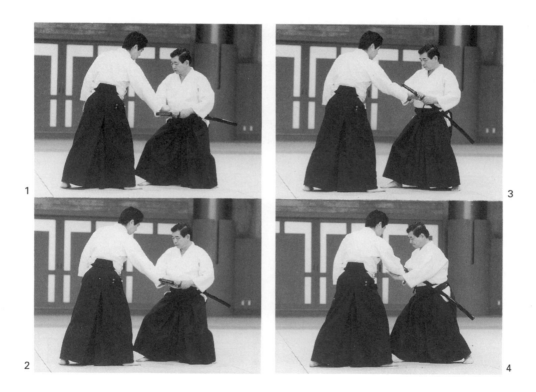

5

6

7

Tachi-dori sanka-jō

Uke grabs *tori*'s right wrist with his right hand, attempting to prevent *tori* drawing his sword. *Tori* twists his hips slightly to the right, breaks *uke*'s hold, and grips *uke*'s wrist in the *sanka-jō* lock. *Tori* applies pressure to *uke*'s wrist, causing *uke* to rise up on his toes as if floating. *Tori* then draws his sword and slashes across *uke*'s body.

5

6

7

8

Kasa-dori shihō-nage

Uke grabs *tori*'s *kasa* (paper umbrella) with his right hand. *Tori* grabs *uke*'s right wrist with his right hand and applies *shihō-nage*, as shown.

5

6

7

Kasa-dori aiki-nage

Uke grabs *tori*'s *kasa* with his right hand. *Tori* pulls down lightly on the *kasa*, takes a large stride forward with his right leg, and throws *uke* to the ground by applying *aiki-age* followed by *aiki-sage*.

4

5

6

Jō-dori futari-nage

Two *uke* hold the *jō* (four-foot staff), one gripping it at either end. *Tori* grips the center of the *jō* with his right hand. He pulls down slightly on it, then pulls it sharply up and then down with a sweeping motion. *Tori* places his right knee on the *jō* and drives it down toward the legs of both *uke*, knocking them off balance. He then pulls up on the *jō* and throws *uke* backward.

2

1

3

4

5

6

Jō-gatame (1)

Uke makes a thrust with the *jō*. *Tori* steps with his right leg to the inside of the attack, grabs the *jō* with his left hand, then takes *uke*'s right wrist and applies a *yonka-jō* lock. *Tori* then steps in with his left leg, places the *jō* against *uke*'s right elbow, and applies pressure to bring *uke* to the ground. *Tori* steps on the *jō* to complete the technique.

5

6

7

8

9

10

Jō-gatame (2)

Uke grabs the end of the *jō* with his left hand. *Tori* rotates the *jō* to the outside of *uke*'s wrist and across *uke*'s elbow, applying pressure downward as he makes a big sweeping turn to bring *uke* to the ground. *Tori* then completes the technique by stepping on the *jō*.

5

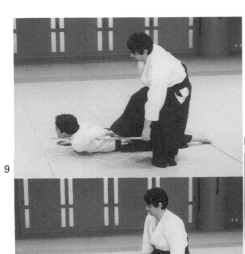

6

7

8

9

10

11

GLOSSARY

aiki	Lit., "blending of *ki*"; harmonized energy.
Aiki Jujutsu	Body techniques based on the application of *aiki* principles.
aiki jūmon	A tenfold division of *aiki* techniques.
aiki o kakeru	To apply *aiki* in a technique.
aiki two-sword principle (style)	Employing both hand-swords to deliver simultaneous blows to pressure points on an opponent's neck and wrist.
aiki-age	Raising the hands upward to break an opponent's balance; designated the "fire-dragon" movement in the Daitoryu.
aiki-sage	Lowering the hands to the side to break an opponent's balance; designated the "water-dragon" movement in the Daitoryu.
Aikido	Lit., "way of harmony"; the way of harmonized *ki*. A discipline founded by Morihei Ueshiba after he spent several decades undergoing severe spiritual and physical forms of training including extensive study of Daitoryu techniques under Sokaku Takeda.
atemi	Blow or kick delivered to any of the body's pressure points.
budō	Lit., "martial ways." Martial arts.
chinkon mudra	Meditative hand movement that can also be used as a martial technique.
Daitoryu	Secret martial art tradition practiced by samurai of the Aizu domain and introduced to the modern world by master Sokaku Takeda beginning at the start of the twentieth century.
Daitoryu Aiki Jujutsu method	One of three methods of performing any technique; this one combines *atemi* with *aiki* timing.

Daitoryu Aiki no Jutsu method	One of three methods of performing any technique; this one relies mainly on *aiki* timing.
Daitoryu Jujutsu method	One of three methods of performing any technique; this one relies primarily on *atemi*.
dō	Way; spiritual path.
dōjō	Training hall.
dokko	Pressure point on the neck below the ear; pressure is applied here at the beginning of *irimi-nage*.
en no sabaki	Circular movement executed by pivoting on one foot to neutralize or redirect an attack.
fudō daiji	Technique based on the tips of the thumbs as the focal point.
fudō no dō	Lit., "immovable movement"; any technique that involves moving a part of one's body while keeping another part immobile.
fudō shōji	Technique based on the tips of the little fingers as the focal point.
fūkaku den	Techniques for bringing the opponent down by attacking his center, grasping his arm at the elbow and pushing it in toward his ear or nose.
funazoko kuden	An aid to the effective application of certain techniques such as *rokka-jō*, in which the arm sweeps along in an arc shape, as if one were scooping water out of the bottom of a rounded boat.
godenkō	Pressure point on the neck.
goka-jō	"Pin number five"; basic Aiki Jujutsu pinning technique.
guinomi kuden	"Saké cup" motion.
hand-sword	The hand turned so that it cuts "like a knife" and so that its edge, including the extended little finger, can be used to deliver a strike or apply a pin.
hanmi	Fighting posture; triangular stance.
hanmi, left	Triangular combative stance with left foot forward and right foot in back.
hanmi, right	Triangular combative stance with right foot forward and left foot in back.
happō	"Eight-direction–throw." See also *karyū happō*.
hara	"Belly"; center of gravity; physical and spiritual center of the human body.
ikka-jō	"Pin number one"; the most basic Aiki Jujutsu pinning technique.

in'yō no den	The "yin-yang" movement; a movement of the palm during a throw, in which the palm faces up at the start of the throw, and down by the end.
irimi	The principle of "entering"; a decisive step forward to neutralize an attack.
irimi-nage	Entering throw.
jō	Four-foot fighting staff.
jujutsu	Body techniques based on the principle of flexibility.
jutsu	Art; technique; martial art.
kaeshi-waza	Reversal techniques; techniques for countering an opponent's technique.
kaishō no den	Movement involving spreading the fingers widely when the wrist is grasped.
kamae	Stance; the posture assumed at the beginning of a technique.
kannuki kuden	"Bolt" lock. An aid to the effective application of *yonka-jō*, this involves keeping your arm straight and directing all your force onto the base of your index finger.
karyū happō	"Fire-dragon eight-direction throw." See also *happō*.
kasa	Paper umbrella.
katame	Pinning methods.
Kendo	Japanese sword-fighting art practiced with protective gear and bamboo swords.
kesa-giri	Diagonal strike across the body.
ki	Life force.
kiai	Spirited yell; also, the state of being fully energized by *ki*.
ki no musubi	The techniques of blending *ki*.
kimeru	To pin decisively.
kote-gaeshi	Wrist lock followed by a throw.
kyokuchi	Pressure point near the elbow.
ma-ai	Combative distance between *tori* and *uke*.
musubi	Creative energy; generative life force.
myaku-mochi no den	"Pulse" hold; to grab the opponent's pulse and twist his arm.
neko no te kuden	"Cat's paw" grip; a technique that allows your own hand to remain completely flexible even while it is being gripped by the opponent.
nonaka no maku kuden	Movement that makes good use of a point of contact established between one's body and the body of an opponent.

nika-jō	"Pin number two"; basic wrist and elbow lock.
obigurai no den	"Belt level"; positioning an opponent's hand at belt level to apply the *kote-gaeshi* technique.
o-shiki-uchi	"Practice in the room." A term by which the Daitoryu teachings were known from about the seventeenth century, which suggests the jealousy with which they were guarded from outsiders.
oguruma	Arm lock.
o-tome bujutsu	"Inside-the-clan martial art." An early term for various martial arts, including the Daitoryu, thought to suggest the secrecy with which the tradition was guarded.
rokka-jō	"Pin number six"; a basic reverse elbow lock.
sanka-jō	"Pin number three"; basic wrist and hand lock.
seiza	Formal kneeling posture.
sensei	Teacher, master.
shihō-nage	Four-direction throw.
shinki	"Divine spirit"; the purest, most elevated form of *ki*.
Shinto	Japan's indigenous religion.
shōkai	Pressure point near the elbow.
shōmen	The crown of the head, or the face between the eyes.
shōmen-uchi	Strike to the crown of the head, or to the face between the eyes.
tantra	Hindu and Buddhist esoteric teachings and ritual instructions on utilizing the body's full potential.
Tao	Life force in ancient Chinese Taoist teaching.
tenchi no den	Lit., "heaven/earth" movement. A specific way of grasping the opponent's hand in *shihō-nage*, so that your index finger is pointing upward (toward "heaven") at the beginning of the throw, and downward (toward earth) by the end.
tori	Person who responds to an attack.
tsuribari kuden	"Fishhook" hold.
tsurizao kuden	"Fishing pole" lock. A light but effective way of gripping an opponent's hand.
uke	Person who initiates an attack.
ukemi	Breakfall; used to escape injury when receiving a technique.

umō no den	"Feathery touch." The use of a light, open-handed touch to guide an opponent's head (or arm) downward.
waza	Technique.
Yoga	Indian system of gymnastics and health-promoting exercises; also, the philosophy of mind-body integration.
yōkei	Pressure point near the wrist.
yōkoku	Pressure point near the wrist.
yokomen	The side of the head.
yokomen-uchi	Strike to the side of the head.
yonka-jō	"Pin number four"; wrist lock applied to the opponent's pulse.